NODIRA AND UVAYSIY

SELECTED POEMS

NODIRA
AND
UVAYSIY

SELECTED POEMS

translated by
Andrew Staniland
with Nazeela Elmi
and Aidakhon Bumatova

published 2022 by
Andrew Staniland's Books

www.andrewstaniland.co.uk

ISBN 9798846503649

Us and our praise of him, his face a rose,
Maknuna, nothing but for these
in this divan of ours.

Nodira

The art of poetry, that is
amongst your mysteries, to its
succinct, affecting pearls of wit,
may I, Uvaysiy, be devoted.

Uvaysiy

Contents

Illustrations

Introduction

Nodira was one of the pen names of Mohlaroyim, who was born in 1792, in an aristocratic and cultured family in the Ferghana Valley, in what is now Uzbekistan, in the city of Andijan, where her father was the governor. Her parents made sure that their daughter had a good education.

In 1808, she married Umar Khan, the younger brother of Alim Khan, the Khan of Kokand. The marriage was intended to reinforce the power of the ruling family, by its alliance with another prominent family. This meant that Nodira had a status of her own, from her family of birth, not merely from being Umar Khan's wife and later, more importantly, his widow.

In 1810, Umar Khan led an uprising against his brother and ordered his assassination, becoming Khan of Kokand himself. His reign was a time of military expansion, but also of cultural flowering. With Umar Khan and Nodira both poets, the court was something of a literary salon. Numerous poets, women as well as men, enjoyed the court's patronage, with Uvaysiy (see below) foremost among the women poets. The court also played an important role in encouraging people throughout the Ferghana Valley to read and write poetry. Nodira and Uvaysiy, in particular, were inspirational examples throughout the nineteenth century for the many women poets at all levels of society.

Umar Khan's reign, though, was a short one. He became ill at the end of 1821 and died in January 1822. He was succeeded by his eldest son, Madali Khan, only about 12 at the time of his father's death. Nodira advised the young Khan and may have done much of the actual business of ruling herself, especially at the start of his reign. She continued to be a great patron of artists and scholars and was also known for her philanthropy. Mosques and madrasas, bazaars and caravanserais were built on her orders.

Madali Khan continued his father's military successes and wrote poetry, like his parents. He ignored his mother's advice, though. He exiled or executed advisers who displeased him and exiled other Kokand noblemen he didn't trust, including his younger brother, Sultan Mahmud Khan. He lost popular support too, because of his heavy drinking (his father also drank, but was much more discreet about it), gambling, drug-taking and worst of all, in the eyes of public opinion, marrying his father's fourth wife. This gave the Emir of Bukhara a pretext to invade. On the brink of defeat, Nodira brokered a deal whereby Madali Khan would share the Khanate with his exiled brother, but Madali didn't honour the deal. In 1842, the Bukharan army marched on Kokand. Many of the soldiers in Madali's army fled and the citizens did nothing to defend him. Sultan Mahmud returned to Kokand to try to save the day, but it was too late. The Bukharan army overran the city and ransacked the palace. Madali Khan, Sultan Mahmud and Nodira were all executed.

Nodira was a bilingual poet. Of the 600 or so poems of hers that have survived, the majority (more than 350) are in Persian. The rest are in Chagatai, the old Turkic language out of which modern Uzbek developed. She wrote mainly *ghazals*, but also many other forms of classical Persian and Turkic poetry, the literature of which she knew well. There are poems of hers that quote or respond to poems by Hafez, Sa'di, Navoiy, Bedil and others.

۶.

Uvaysiy was the pen name of Jahon Otin, who was born in 1779, also in a cultured family in the Ferghana Valley, in her case in Margilan. Her parents, as Nodira's did a few years later, made sure their daughter had a good education. Her father was a poet himself and her mother was an Otin, a female religious teacher, a Sufi wise woman. Uvaysiy became both a poet and an Otin.

Uvaysiy's husband also died young. After his death, Nodira and Umar Khan invited her to Kokand, to live in their palace and teach their children. She played a leading role in the literary life there, teaching, writing and promoting poetry. After Umar Khan's death, Nodira and Uvaysiy went on writers' tours to Andijan, Khojand, Tashkent and other cities, to meet poets there and establish a literary network in the region.

Uvaysiy had a daughter and a son, both of whom died before she did. After the Bukharan army's conquest of Kokand and Nodira's execution, she retired to Margilan until her own death in 1845.

The 350-400 of Uvaysiy's poems that have survived are all in Chagatai, but she was as well-versed as Nodira in Persian as well as Turkic literature. She wrote poems that respond to poems by Navoiy, Jami, Fuzuli and others. Her *diwans* (collections) again contain mainly *ghazals*, as well as other forms, including three *dastans* (narrative or epic poems), two about important figures from Islamic history and one, incomplete, about Madali Khan.

Otins since Uvaysiy, especially in the Ferghana Valley, have recited and continue to recite her poems at ceremonial gatherings of women, where Nodira's poems may also be recited.

❧

The poems in this selection are *ghazals*, *chistons*, two *ruba'iyat*, a *tarjiband*, one stanza from a *mukhammas* and a *dastan* (in spirit only). Nodira's Persian and Chagatai

3

poetry are both represented, in approximately the same proportion as those that have survived.

A *ghazal* is a type of poem which originated in Arabic poetry and was developed in Persian poetry. For example, the tradition of including the poet's name in the final couplet was a Persian addition. Each couplet is actually two half-lines (hemistichs) of one long line. Both hemistichs of the first couplet have either a refrain preceded by a rhyme or simply a rhyme, repeated in the second hemistich of all the following couplets. The couplets are all independent, variations on a theme, with no continuity from one couplet to the next.

A *chiston* is a riddle. *Ruba'i, tarjiband* and *mukhammas* are explained in the Notes on each of them.

&

The translations are by English poet Andrew Staniland, with the help of Nazeela Elmi and Aidakhon Bumatova. Nazeela and Aida provided literal translations of the originals, explanations of the meaning and feedback on drafts of the English verse settings. They are as faithful as possible to the originals, though inevitably a translation into a new language becomes a new poem.

As an ethnic Uzbek from Afghanistan, Nazeela is a native speaker of both Uzbek and Persian, so Nodira's poems in Persian, unjustly neglected despite being the majority, were as available for translation as those in Chagatai, and in the original Persian script, rather than only in Cyrillic transliterations. Nazeela's family also helped, especially with the Chagatai poems. In Afghanistan, Uzbek has always been taught in the family, rather than at school.

Aida speaks Tajik as well as Uzbek, so she was able to translate three Persian poems that were only available in Cyrillic texts. She had already co-translated twelve of

Alisher Navoiy's *ghazals* with Andrew, for the book *12 Ghazals By Alisher Navoiy, 14 Poems By Abdulhamid Cho'lpon*, and translated five of Uvaysiy's *ghazals* here as well.

ﻉ

The original poems are in *aruz* metre, which uses long and short syllables as its measure, the same as the metre of Ancient Greek poetry. What structures speech in English, though, isn't syllable length, it is syllable stress, so when classical metre was introduced to English poetry, stressed and unstressed syllables was the measure used. This is the metre used in the translations and is predominantly iambic (i.e. unstressed-stressed).

The length of the lines often varies within the poems, especially Nodira's. The translations have the same flexibility, though lines are usually no more than a syllable longer than the original. They look longer because English uses more letters and *doesn'tstick wordstogether* (Persian has unwritten vowels too). Lines of seven or more beats have been stepped at the caesura (a caesura is a break in a line of verse, used in long lines like the support in the middle of a bridge that has two spans), as have lines of six beats that would have run onto the next line on the page anyway. Here is an example, with the stressed syllables in bold and a trochee (stressed-unstressed) in the final half-line:

On **that** day **of** e**ter**nity,
      I **heard** the **se**cret **of** its **wine**.
Today, my **heart** is, **ah**, a **back**-
      water and **it** is **boil**ing **o**ver.

Where the original poems have refrains preceded by a rhyme, the translations only have a refrain, as English is much more specific in its rhymes.

In both Chagatai and Persian, multiple rhymes are readily available. Often, they are more like refrains at the end of words, repeating, for example, the same inflection, possessive or preposition. The regularity of verb endings means that every verb is available as a rhyme with every other verb. This would be true in English if the stress was on the last syllable in *running, jumping, swimming*, which it obviously isn't. Similarly, the addition of regular plural endings, possessives and prepositional suffixes (postpositions) to the end of nouns and pronouns means that every noun and pronoun is available as a rhyme with every other one. For example, as constructed in Chagatai or Persian and with the stress in bold, *hous**es*** and *bridg**es***, *heart**my*** and *head**my*** or *heartthe**from*** and *them**from***.

In English, rhymes are much more forceful. The stress, which they depend on, is often on the root of the word (**meet**ing and **greet**ing rhyme, **jump**ing and **swimm**ing don't) and there are fewer to choose from. A *ghazal* with eleven couplets, for example, has the same rhyme twelve times in the original (twice in the first couplet). In English, this is almost impossible and at best would be strained and obtrusive, unlike the originals. What was more important was to translate the usefulness and fluency that are essential characteristics of a *ghazal*. Nodira and Uvaysiy both wrote hundreds of them.

ِ۔

There were no printing presses in Central Asia in their lifetimes, so their collections were copied by hand. For this book, the original poems and the translations are on facing pages. The Persian poems are shown in Persian-Arabic script, except those which were only available in Cyrillic. Chagatai, though, at least in what is now Uzbekistan, has had four different scripts since these poems were written. In the nineteenth century, it was written in Arabic script. In the twentieth century, it changed as the script of modern Uzbek changed, first to the *Yan Alif* Latin script, then to Cyrillic, then to modern Latin, though Cyrillic is still widely used. Among Afghan Uzbeks, in contrast, the original Arabic script is still used today for both Uzbek and Chagatai (though the translators didn't have access to any of the nineteenth century manuscripts). The Chagatai poems here are shown in modern Latin script, so an English reader can see the elements of them, such as rhymes and refrains.

ﻉﻼ

There are no contemporary portraits of Nodira or Uvaysiy. For the illustrations, Naima Muminiy has drawn on the traditions of Central Asian miniature painting to give a stylised representation.

The monument on Nodira's grave, similarly stylised in the illustration here, is in the graveyard of the Narbutabey mosque and madrasa in Kokand and dates from the Soviet period, when Nodira's remains were moved from the Modari Khan mausoleum to dissociate her from the feudal rulers buried there. The palace in Kokand that can also be seen today, a detail of which is shown on the cover, was built in about 1871 by a later khan, Khudayar Khan, a son of one of Umar Khan's cousins, on the site of the razed palace of Madali Khan.

Uvaysiy has a house museum in Margilan, a modern building but with her grave, a plain brick semi-cylinder (as Nodira's original grave was), in the courtyard.

SELECTED POEMS

Uvaysiy

Ul na gumbazdur: eshigi, tuynugidin yoʻq nishon,
Necha gulgunpoʻsh qizlar manzil aylabdur makon.
Sindurub gumbazni, qizlar holidin olsam xabar,
Yuzlarida parda tortigʻliq, turarlar bagʻri qon.

A Riddle

There is a dome, there is no door,
                    no daylight, not a chink,
And there are many women there
                    and they are all in pink.
I open up the dome and ask
                    the women how they are.
They are all veiled. And an embrace
                    and there is blood to drink.

Uvaysiy

اي بهار جلوه خرّم از نهال قامتت
ديده ها محو تماشا از وصال قامتت

خوبي و موزوني و آزادگي و دلكشي
هست مضموني ز مكتوب مآل قامتت

چون تو نخلي در بهارستان خوبي كس نديد
سرو با شمشاد يك سر پايمال قامتت

نسخه ي آزادگي پيداست از هر مصرع ام
بس كه دارم در سخن فكر و خيال قامتت

سروقدان جهان را سال ها ديديم، نيست
در ميان نازپيرايان مثال قامتت

گرچه هجران هر زماني تازه داغم مي كند
شوق ها دارم ز اميد وصال قامتت

ناله ي قُمري بود از سرو فرياد ملال
در گلستاني كه بالد اعتدال قامتت

سال ها شد هست مقصود و مرام، اي مه جبين
بگذرد در شادكامي ماه و سال قامتت

تا بهارستان عالم هست سرسبز اينچنين
سربلندي باد همدوش كمال قامتت

14

O spring, how sweet it is to see your sapling's stature
　　approaching me, my eyes astonished by that stature.

　　　　　　　　　　　　　　ଈ

Refinement and proportion and
　　　　　　　　　　　　insouciance and handsomeness
　　are subjects of a letter that concerns your stature.

　　　　　　　　　　　　　　ଈ

No one has seen a palm tree in
　　　　　　　　　　　　the land of spring that is your equal,
　　a cypress or a boxwood tree
　　　　　　　　　　　　not stamped on by your stature.

　　　　　　　　　　　　　　ଈ

In any line that I am writ-
　　　　　　　　　　　　ing, there is something that is free,
　　from thinking of you, from imagining your stature.

　　　　　　　　　　　　　　ଈ

We have seen men as tall as cypresses, not one,
　　amongst the whole world's beaux,
　　　　　　　　　　　　　　to set against your stature.

　　　　　　　　　　　　　　ଈ

Although your absences all scorch me, I have hope
　　too, from anticipating your approaching stature.

　　　　　　　　　　　　　　ଈ

A dove says no to nesting in
　　　　　　　　　　　　a cypress when it sees you in
　　the garden spreading out like wings
　　　　　　　　　　　　your well-proportioned stature.

　　　　　　　　　　　　　　ଈ

بر مرام آرزو در شوکت حسن وفا
چشم اندازم که آید راست فال قامتت

گشت آخر در چمنزار مضامین کمال
فطرت مکنونه موزون از خیال قامتت

For many years, my moon-faced one,
                      what I have worked for is
    that any month and any year
                  will satisfy your stature.

ક

As long as, in the garden of
                  the universe, it is this green,
    may your head be held high
                  by your accomplished stature.

ક

Making a wish for that
                fidelity that is so fine,
    I set my eyes on seeing your auspicious stature.

ક

Maknuna, in the meadow of maturity,
    has equanimity from thinking of your stature.

Nodira

Maqsudi ko'ngul — la'li mayi nobinga qulman,
Andin sochilan ul duri noyobinga qulman.

El sajda qilur masjid devorig'a har dam,
O'lguncha bosh omon, qoshi mehrobinga qulman.

Bilmasligim ifshosin eshitmakligim uchun
Baxtim kabi ul kokuli qullobinga qulman.

Rutbangki falak toqida, ey badri saodat,
Zotingga yetolmay, seni mahtobinga qulman.

Bu dahr aro tush kabi umrimni kechurdim,
Nechun ochilur bilmagan ul xobinga qulman.

Vaysiy bu Jahon amricha ish qildi tun-u kun,
To aydi jahon Vaysiyg'a: "Odobinga qulman!"

To the sweet wine of your lips, my
      soul's goal, I am a slave.
To the pure pearls that pour from those
      sweet lips, I am a slave.

❦

A mosque wall is what we all bow
      before. Thus is it that,
before an eyebrow's *mihrab*, while
      I live, I am a slave.

❦

Not knowing when a smile of some
      good fortune will be mine,
it is a lucky lock of hair
      to which I am a slave.

❦

That haunt of yours, in heaven's heights,
      O moon of my delight,
is out of reach for me. To you,
      my sun, I am a slave.

❦

Watching my worldly life go by,
      as if it is a dream,
I don't know how to wake up. To
      this sleep, I am a slave.

❦

Uvaysiy, day and night, did what
the world told her to do,
so the world said to Vaysiy, "To
dutiful you, I am a slave!"

Uvaysiy

Marhabo, ey payki sulton, marhabo,
Hudhudi mulki Sulaymon, marhabo.

Tal'ating farrux, muborak maqdaming
Qildi kulbamni guliston, marhabo.

Xo'b kelding, yaxshi keltirding xabar,
Aylading dardimga darmon, marhabo.

Bo'ldi mavzun qomatingdin munfail,
Sarvi nozi bog'i rizvon, marhabo.

Qilg'asen ul moh mehrin oshkor,
Subh yanglig' pokdomon, marhabo.

Mujda keltirding visoli yordin,
Topti taskin dardi hijron, marhabo.

Kel beri, to xoki poyingni qilay
To'tiyoyi chashmi giryon, marhabo.

Ravshan aylarman chirog'i ohni,
Ko'zlarimdur gavharafshon, marhabo.

Bu kecha hijron shabistonidadur
Anjumi ashkim charog'on, marhabo.

Qo'y kafi poyingni diydam ustina
Bir dam, ey sarvi xiromon, marhabo.

Nodira, har so'zki insho ayladim,
Aydi anga ahli davron: "Marhabo!"

Welcome, O envoy of the Sultan, welcome,
Solomon's hoopoe, from his kingdom, welcome!

❧

Whose face is blissful and whose footsteps blessed,
so these bare grounds become a garden, welcome!

❧

Who comes well, who comes carrying good news
and has the cure for what afflicts me, welcome!

❧

Whose stature is so shapely and so straight
that Rizwan's cypress has been humbled, welcome!

❧

That moon that shows his love to me
and is as chaste as dawn is, welcome!

❧

Who brings good news of our reunion,
so I find solace for my longing, welcome!

❧

Come closer, so the dust upon your feet
is decorated by my weeping, welcome!

❧

These gems that I am casting from my eyes
bring brightness to my "ah"s of anguish, welcome!

❧

Tonight, in my bedchamber, where the lights
　　of tears illuminate my longing, welcome!

ؔ

Setting those soles, a second only, on
　　my eyes, O softly-stepping cypress, welcome!

ؔ

Through all these lines that I, Nodira, write,
　　the people of our era bid you, "Welcome!"

Nodira

Ul nadurkim, sabzto'nlik, yoz yog'ochning boshida,
Qish yalang'och aylagay barcha xaloyiq qoshida.
Barcha qushlarning so'ngoki ichida,
Ul na qushdurkim, so'ngoki toshida.

Ikki mahbubni ko'rdum, bir-birisin ko'rmagan,
Ikkisining o'rtasiga, do'stlar, qil sig'magan.

Two Riddles

A green man is what he is, in midsummer, on a tree.
In winter, he is naked (and in public) on a tray.

A bird's bones in a shell is what we see,
A bird, its bones still in a shell, is he.

 familia

I see a couple who don't see
     each other face to face.
Between the two of them, my friends,
      is not a hair of space.

Uvaysiy

Nega arbobi xirad ahli junundan ori bor?
Kim bular uryon alarning jubbayi dastori bor.

Gul yuzung olida zohir qildi shabnamdin araq,
G'uncha xomushu labingni gavhari guftori bor.

Bo'lma mahzun bog'bon, bog'ingga kirmas mahvashim,
Sarvdur qaddi ani, ruxsoridin gulzori bor.

Soqiyo, may birla bir soat meni shodon qil,
Notavon ko'nglumni hijron dardidan ozori bor.

Ey ko'ngul, diningni pinhon asra ishq atvorida,
Qoshini har bir xamida ko'z degan ayyori bor.

Ko'hkan Shiringa oshiq bo'ldi, Majnun Layliga,
Kim muhabbat shahrida har kimsani bir yori bor.

Rishtayi zulfini bo'ynumda ko'rub ta'n aylamang,
Bir birahman but yo'lida bo'ynida zunnori bor.

Yor ishqidin parilar e'tiroz aylar magar,
Har birini bo'ynida ta'viz ila tummori bor.

Dilrabolar ichra yaktoliqqa mashhur o'lsa, lek
Ko'yida men telba yanglig' benihoyat zori bor.

Ey pari, bir kun buzuq kulbam sari qilg'il xirom,
Hech agar yo'qtur zamoni soyayi devori bor.

Ne sababdin o'lmasun obod ko'nglum kishvari,
Ishq shohidek Amiri ma'dilat osori bor.

Why are wise men embarrassed by
　　　　love's lunacy, as they all are?
　　They won't run naked. Those long, so-
　　　　　　　ber robes they wear are who they are.

　　　　　　　　ه

　　A breath of dew dawned in the air
　　　　　　　　before the rose that is your face.
　　　Rosebuds are silent. Only on
　　　　　　　your lips is where word-jewels are.

　　　　　　　　ه

Do not be sad, my moonlike one,
　　　　that in your garden will not go
　　the gardener, of cypress height,
　　　　his face a field where flowers are.

　　　　　　　　ه

　　Cupbearer, come here, make me happy
　　　　　　　　for an hour. How much it hurts
　　　this feeble heart to be bereft,
　　　　　　　this is what all these heartaches are.

　　　　　　　　ه

O heart, hide your belief from harm
　　　　beneath how you behave in love.
　　A cunning cover for the eyes
　　　　is what the eyebrows, archly, are.

　　　　　　　　ه

That mountain miner loved Shirin.
                    Majnun loved Layla. In
    love's city, those who live there are
                    someone's beloved. They all are.

                    ঽ৶

The lock of hair around my neck
            should not be a surprise to you.
    It is what brahmins wear for their
            own idols, what their *zunnars* are.

                    ঽ৶

The *peris* would complain as well
                    of their beloved's love but for
    the amulets around their necks,
            where spells that they have written are.

                    ঽ৶

What heartthrobs are renowned for is
            that they are all the only one,
    with supplicants as mad as me,
            and numberless is what these are.

                    ঽ৶

One of these days, O *peri*, wan-
                    der over to my ruined home.
    Although there may be nothing there,
            it has a wall where shadows are.

                    ঽ৶

31

A happy country of the heart
    will be built here, if this is where
Amiriy is, the Shah of Love,
    where monuments of justice are.

Amiriy & Nodira

Chiqib ishq o'ti ko'ksim chokidin, boshimdin oshibdur,
Quruq shoxeki, go'yo o'z ichidin o't tutoshibdur.

Ko'zing jon labga yetkurdi, labing jon qo'shti jonimg'a,
Bu ikki do'stlar ul joni mahzunim taloshibdur.

Azal kunda asar etgandi sirri may qulog'img'a,
Bugun, vah, dil bulog'l jo'sh urmoqliqda toshibdur.

Visoling orzusi shiddati hijronni yiqmoqda,
Bu ikki pahlavon maydoni dil uzra kuroshibdur.

Uvaysiy, olma boshing zikru fikri yor yodidin,
Suluki ishq aro be yodi haq yo'ldin odoshibdur.

It was my heart that love broke out
      of and my head that it bowed over,
  as if I was a dry branch that
        its flames burst out of and blazed over.

ﻌ

Those eyes! My soul was on my lips...
      Those lips! And in my soul, more soul,
  a sad soul these two friends of mine
        were working over, working over.

ﻌ

On that day of eternity,
      I heard the secret of its wine.
  Today, my heart is, ah, a back-
        water and it is boiling over.

ﻌ

Thinking of being with you and
      being bereft without you, these
  two, in that wrestling ring, my heart,
        throw one another over and over.

ﻌ

Uvaysiy, do not lose yourself
      in *zikr* that is on some one
  and not on God. If you do that,
        the way of love will soon grow over.

Uvaysiy

35

Навбаҳор аст, санавбар зада бар сар гули сурх,
Тоҷи заррин зада бар фарқи санавбар гули сурх.

Шишаи ғунча лаболаб зи гулоб аст имрӯз,
Баски шуд об зи шарми рухи дилбар гули сурх.

Файзи гулгашти чаман нашъаи дигар дорад,
Ҳар тараф ғунча сабӯ дораду соғар гули сурх.

Муждаи айшу тараб мерасад аз боди баҳор,
Боз дар саҳни гулистон зада чодар гули сурх.

Ҳар куҷо ашк фишондам, дамад он ҷо гули зард,
Ту ба ҳар ҷо, ки ниҳӣ пой, кашад сар гули сурх.

То ба кай ҷилваи гулзор таманно кардан,
Рез, Макнуна, кунун аз мижаи тар гули сурх.

Spring! So the cypresses
   have crowned their heads with red, red roses.
  This cypress has a crown of gold
     instead of red, red roses.

    ‽

The water in this vase is rose-
    water. The reason why
  is spying my beloved's eye
    dissolved the red, red roses.

    ‽

Wandering round this garden, I
    am giddy and unsteady.
  The buds are little jugs of wine,
    the cups are red, red roses.

    ‽

The spring wind spreads glad tidings with
     the raindrops that it brings.
  Flourishing in the flowerbeds
    again are red, red roses.

    ‽

Wherever I shed tears on them,
    the roses all grow yellow.
  Wherever you, on tiptoes, tread,
    "ah" go the red, red roses.

    ‽

How long have you here to enjoy
                    this garden's gorgeousness?
        Maknuna, from your sodden eye-
                        lashes shed red, red roses.

Nodira

Dunyoni bugun davr ila davroni g'animat,
Kelturdi xaloyiqniki mehmoni g'animat.

To bulbuli mastona suxanrezni bul dam,
Ayvoni jahon bog'i gulistoni g'animat.

Bu shavkatu sha'ningni xudoyim nasib etsun,
Davlat nigini, taxti Sulaymoni g'animat.

Umringni bahorida muhabbatni sug'org'il,
Ko'z mardumini giryai boroni g'animat.

Ochgil ko'zing, ey dil, qilako'r vaqti tamosho,
Ayyomi jahoni mahi toboni g'animat.

Fazli bila ul g'unchai nashkufta ochilmish,
Sayri chamani ham guli xandoni g'animat.

Vaysiyi gado, sen bu kun o'ksitma gadoni,
Lutf ila tarahhum yana ehsoni g'animat.

The hour that it is now on earth,
      the era, are our bounty.
A feast that we are guests at, His
      creation is our bounty.

&ea.

While ever giddy nightingales
      string words out, note by note,
the *iwan* of the earth, the beds
      where buds bloom are our bounty.

&ea.

May you be granted grandeur, grant-
      ed graciousness by God.
Solomon's seat of state, a crown
      of crystals are your bounty.

&ea.

Love is for you to water in
      the seedtime of your life.
The apple of your eye and its
      spring showers are your bounty.

&ea.

Open your eyes, O heart, and see
      how splendid this time is.
These days on earth, the dazzle of
      a round moon are our bounty.

&ea.

A bud, too tight-lipped, through His grace,
      has bloomed. To see its bed
and see that bud, become a rose
      now, smiling, is our bounty.

ॐ

Poor Vaysiy, do no ill deed to
      a poor soul you will meet today.
Caring and being kind and do-
      ing good deeds are our bounty.

Uvaysiy

در وصالت خاطر ما شاد باد
مرغ دل از دام غم آزاد باد

خانه ي دل جلوه گاه ناز اوست
تا قيامت اين بنا آباد باد

عشرت جاويد بر كف داشتي
اي دل، از بزم وصالش ياد باد

چشم و دل در دامگاه بيخودي
واله آن سرو حوري زاد باد

در محبت عجز ميآيد به كار
خرمن حرص و هوا بر باد باد

تا كشد بار ملامت را به دوش
با ضعيفان از غمت امداد باد

كرده ام مكنونه در شب ناله ها
در خيالت هرچي بادا باد باد!

To be one and be happy, may that be.
　　Hearts that are free from snares of sorrow, may that be.

ﻉ

A bridal chamber of seduction in the heart,
　　until the Day of Judgement, may that be.

ﻉ

The endless pleasures you had in your hands, O heart,
　　that you remember feasting on them, may that be.

ﻉ

My eyes, my heart, in a circus of self-loss,
　　that cypress-*houri* sighing, may that be.

ﻉ

We gain by giving in to our beloved. That
　　the wind blows lust away
　　　　　　　　like threshed chaff, may that be.

ﻉ

That you will save the one who suffers for you and
　　bears all the blame on her weak shoulders, may that be.

ﻉ

Maknuna, be it what it may that your
　　nocturnal sighs imagine, may that be.

Nodira

Meni rasvo qilan kimdirki, sen siyminbadan nozuk,
Solan boshimg'a savdo kimdur, ul gul pirohan nozuk.

Xayoli kirsa ko'nglumga chiqar dunyo-u din mehri,
Qilibdur oqibat, ey do'stlar, ham bevatan nozuk.

Chu sabrim tirnog'ida har kuni yuz ko'hi g'am qozdim,
Meni oldimdadur Farhod — ojiz, Ko'hkan nozuk.

Qading nozuk, qoshing nozuk, ko'zung nozuk, labing
                                              nozuk,
Tiling nozuk, so'zung nozuk, tishing durri Adan nozuk.

Xatingdur sabza rayhoniy , labingdur kavsar andomi,
Mijang — bo'ston, yuzung — gul, misli gulzori chaman
                                              nozuk.

Boshingdin to ayog'ingg'a qarab tursam, baring nozuk,
Xususan g'abg'abing ostida ul zeri zaqan nozuk.

Ikki nargis, ikki ko'ngul, ikki tan, ikki jon birlan,
Birin biriga vasl aylab, qiloli anjuman nozuk.

Uvaysiy, o'z-o'zingcha, so'zlama, tiygil zaboningni,
Mabodo kelmasun nozuk diliga so'z garan nozuk.

That one who brings such shame upon
        me, he is silver-limbed, so fine.
That one with whom my brain has so
        much business, he is flower-fine.

                        ❧

These fantasies that fill my heart
        force out all love of life and faith,
until the little link I have
        to them, my friends, is far too fine.

                        ❧

How patiently I mine through moun-
        tains, hundreds of them, with my nails.
The mountain miner that Farhad
        was, on this scale, was far from fine.

                        ❧

That build, so fine, those eyebrows, fine,
        those eyes, so fine, those lips, so fine,
that tongue, so fine, those words, so fine,
        those teeth, Edenic pearls, so fine.

                        ❧

Sweet basil is the line above
        that lip, that is a brook of heaven.
Eyelashes — bower, face — a flower,
        you are like flower beds, as fine.

                        ❧

Looking at you, from top to toe,
       your figure is so fine,
    under your chin, especially,
        that line of chin and jaw, so fine.

                ه

Two daffodils, we are two hearts,
       two bodies and two souls as one.
    And one to one, in union,
        the conference within is fine.

                ه

Uvaysiy, keep your distance, stop
       yourself from speaking, hold your tongue,
    in case a word of yours seems coarse
        to the fine heart of one so fine.

Uvaysiy

Na gul sayr ayla, na fikri bahor et,
Jahondin kech, xayoli vasli yor et.

Muhabbatsiz kishi odam emasdur,
Gar odamsan, muhabbat ixtiyor et.

Uzoru qaddu raftoringni ko'rsat,
Chaman sarvu gulini sharmisor et.

Labi maxmurdadurmen, jomi may tut,
Karam qil, soqiyo, daf'i humor et.

"Analhaq" mojarosin aylading fosh,
Kel, ey Mansur, istiqboli dor et.

Duru ashku aqiqi xuni dilni,
Kelu yoring ayog'ig'a nisor et.

Kuyib, ey Nodira, olam elig'a
Muhabbat shevasini oshkor et.

Thinking of springtime isn't what to do,
    thinking upon the One is what to do.

꜒

Not loving is to not be human. To
    be human, owning love is what to do.

꜒

Showing how high your stature is, to shame
    the cypress and the rose, is what to do.

꜒

Holding the cup, cupbearer, to my lips
    to help my drunkenness is what to do.

꜒

"I am the Truth" is what was shown by you.
    Greeting the noose, Mansur, is what to do.

꜒

Setting salt pearls and agates of the heart
    at the Companion's feet is what to do.

꜒

Nodira, burning brightly, so the world
    will learn the way to love, is what to do.

Nodira

آن ماه به من عتاب دارد
این خانه دل خراب دارد

روشنده ظلمت اسیران
از عارضش آفتاب دارد

با زلف کند به خود مقید
بر گردن دل طناب دارد

از یار به عاشقان ترحم
در غمکده پیچ و تاب دارد

خال و خط او به صفحه‌ی رخ
مضمون دوصد کتاب دارد

مکنونه ز هجر گلع زارش،
چشمان عجب پرآب دارد

The right to reprimand me, that moon holds,
    to ruin this heart's house, it holds.

                    ❧

Bringer of light to a benighted slave,
    the sun's face is what his face holds.

                    ❧

Tying me to him with a lock of hair,
    a noose around my heart is what he holds.

                    ❧

Such sympathy as a beloved has,
    how many twists and turns it holds.

                    ❧

One letter of one look, the contents of
    two hundred books is what it holds.

                    ❧

Maknuna has been banished from his garden.
    See how much water each eye holds.

Nodira

Ikki mahbubni ko'rdum, ikkisin kindigi bir,
Ikkisin orasiga tushsang, topadursan kasir.

⁂

Ul nadurkim, shahdin totlik erur xumorig'a,
Ixtiyor etmas sotarin kirmag'ay bozorg'a.

Two Riddles

I see a couple who have got
                    one navel. One, not two!
And if you cross the two of them,
                         there will be two of you.

                    ঙ১

This one, that we want more of, sweet-
                         er than the honey in a jar,
Is so sweet we won't sell it, we
                    won't go with it to the bazaar.

Uvaysiy

Бе ту дар базми тараб мавҷи шаробам оташ аст,
Бе майи лаъли лабат нуқли шаробам оташ аст.

Васл мушкил, ёр бепарво, фиғонам бе асар,
Дӯстон раҳме, ки дар ҷони харобам оташ аст.

Рост гӯям рӯзу шаб бе ту месӯзам зи ҳаҷр,
Ҳосили бедориам доғ асту хобам оташ аст.

Заҳр бошад бе лаби лаъли ту дар комам набот,
Дурам аз базми ту ҳамчун шамъ обам оташ аст.

Ваҳ, намедонам чӣ сон дар ишқи ту тоб оварам,
Ман гиёҳу дилбари олиҷанобам оташ аст.

Аз табу тоби дили зорам мапурс, эй ҳамнафас,
Шамъи ҳиҷронам, табам доғ асту тобам оташ аст.

Дар каломам нест, Макнуна ба ғайр аз сӯхтан,
Дафтарам маҷмӯаи доғу китобам оташ аст.

Without you to enjoy this ban-
                      quet with, the wine's waves are on fire.
     Without wine from your ruby lips,
                           food is on fire and wine on fire.

                              ❧

We scarcely meet, but my belov-
                      ed doesn't care. It does no good to weep.
     Have mercy, O my friends, my soul,
                              that is in ruins, is on fire.

                              ❧

The truth is, day and night, I am
                      on fire without you. When I am
     awake, I am on fire, and when
                      I am asleep, I am on fire.

                              ❧

Sugar is bitter on my tongue
                      without the sweetness of your lips.
     That banquet, now, is far away.
                      My candle melts and is on fire.

                              ❧

I don't know how it came about,
                      alas, I fell in love with you.
     I am like grass that noble and
                      that charming one has set on fire.

                              ❧

Don't ask me, O my dear, how much
　　　　　　　　　my heart is hurting now.
　　Being bereft besmirches it,
　　　　　　　　a candle in a lamp that is on fire.

　　　　　　　　　ৠ

Maknuna, words of mourning are
　　　　　　　　the only ones I have, my notes
　　are stained by sorrow and
　　　　　　　the body of my poems is on fire.

Nodira

Jafo chekkanlara, jonon, vafolig' qilg'oning yaxshi,
Asiri ishq o'lanlarg'a shifolig' qilg'oning yaxshi.

Dili majruhning zaxmiga marham bersang, ey sayyod,
Xadangingga nishon aylab, yarolig' qilg'oning yaxshi.

Muyassar bo'lsa vasling chunki jon bermakligimdin so'ng,
Tanimdin darmahal jonim judolig' qilg'oning yaxshi.

Meni mahrum etib shahlo ko'zungdin, ey xaridorim,
Meni arzonu, g'aflatni baholig' qilg'oning yaxshi.

Baqosiz bilding endi bu jahon ra'nolarin, ey dil,
Borib mayxona kunjida fanolig' qilg'oning yaxshi.

Bugun yor oldida qo'yg'il, Uvaysiy, sho'ru g'avg'oni,
Xudo qozi bo'lan chog' mojarolig' qilg'oning yaxshi...

That we, my dear, have faith in all
        those who have been betrayed is good,
that we give aid to all those who
        are in the grip of love is good.

        * え*

Either of these, applying balm,
        O hunter, to a wounded heart
or aiming at that target with
        the arrows of your eyes, is good.

        え

Since union with you will be
        attained as soon as I have died,
the separation, right now, of
        my body from my soul is good.

        え

You have withheld the treasure from
        me, O my suitor, of your eyes.
To think I am so cheap that to
        ignore me costs you more is good.

        え

Now that you know the beauty of
        this world is evanescent, O
my heart, to go into an inn
        and seek oblivion is good.

        え

Today, with your beloved friend,
     Uvaysiy, stop this quarrelling.
To wait until the judge of an-
     y argument is God is good.

Uvaysiy

از هجر رخش عذاب دارم
یک پاره دل کباب دارم

از سر نرود هوای مستی
از فکر لبش شراب دارم

از بهررسیدن وصالش
چون برق بسی شتاب دارم

گردانده ز روی شب ورق ها
عمر گذران کتاب دارم

پرسیدن حال درد هجران
جرمی نبود، صواب دارم

مکنونه ز ظلم فرقت او
دو دیده درون آب دارم

Him turned away torments me. That is what I have.
A heart like some charred meat is what I have.

≈

A constant giddiness, a taste of wine,
from thinking of his lips, is what I have.

≈

To go to him, to be with him again,
a lightning-like alacrity is what I have.

≈

The pages of the night are turning, one by one.
A book of days gone by is what I have.

≈

In telling you my torment, I do nothing wrong.
Doing the right thing, that is what I have.

≈

From his abandonment of me, Maknuna,
two underwater eyes are what I have.

Nodira

Gul emas to boʻlmasa oldida xori koʻndalang,
Yor koʻyi ermas ul, yoʻq dilfigori koʻndalang.

Ul sanam koʻyiga etkayman debon qilma navo,
Yoʻl aro necha saningdek intizori koʻndalang.

Shoʻxlik birla munodi qildirib qon toʻkkali —
Kirsa maydon ichra uldam, shahsuvori koʻndalang.

Har kishi Mansurdek bersa "analhaq"dan xabar,
Ul zamon boʻlgʻay ani oldida dori koʻndalang.

Vaysiy, soʻz koʻtoh qil, dam urma nodonlar aro,
Soʻzni sof etkuicha to chiqmay gʻubori koʻndalang.

A rose is not a rose unless
        some thorns are in the way.
    A heart does not know love unless
        some hurt is in the way.

❧

Don't sing a song that says that you
        are in your idol's house.
    So many like you wait outside
        and they are in the way.

❧

How boisterously blood is gushing,
        how beseechingly.
    Upon the field there is a shah
        in armour in the way.

❧

To anyone announcing like
        Mansur, "I am the Truth,"
    a time will come that on their path
        a noose is in the way.

❧

Uvaysiy, gag your speech before
        you go among the ignorant,
    until each phrase evaporates
        and fog is in the way.

Uvaysiy

Ey gul, jigarim qoni uzoringg'a munosib,
Yuz porali ko'ksum dag'i xoringg'a munosib.

Sarf aylama har bexabara la'li hadisin,
To qahr g'azab ham meni zoringg'a munosib.

Tun sog'arida sharbati bedorlig' ichsang,
Mastonalig' ul chashmi xumoringg'a munosib.

To qildi muattar xati rayhoni sahargoh,
Xushholligim husni bahoringg'a munosib.

Man' etma tarahhum etibon, yor, yo'lungdin,
Ashkim yo'l aro man'i g'uvoringg'a munosib.

Dil manzarini pok etibon muntazir o'ldum,
Bo'lg'oymu ekin tab'i gulzoringg'a munosib?

Rashk otashini, Vaysiy, bugun ayla mukarrar,
Yuz sen kabi devona nigoringg'a munosib.

O rose, the scarlet of my heart,
  of your cheeks is the equal,
the hundred splinters in my breast,
  of your thorns are the equal.

     ða.

Don't hold forth to the ignorant
  with ruby-lipped *hadiths*.
I want to hear you. To your in-
  dignation I am equal.

     ða.

The sleeplessness and drunkenness
  of drinking from the night's
bottomless goblet, of a draught
  of your eyes, are the equal.

     ða.

As dawn diffused the fragrance from
  the down above your lip,
of this, your beauty's springtime, my
  rejoicing is the equal.

     ða.

Don't banish me, beloved, don't
  be merciful. To all
the dust of roaming on your feet
  my weeping will be equal.

     ða.

The garden of my heart, I tend
        with great care while I wait.
    Of yours, so cultivated, will
        it grow to be the equal?

            ॐ

Uvaysiy, of the hundred who
        with your beloved are
    besotted, may this jealousy
        that burns you be the equal.

Uvaysiy

دست قضا که رونق باغ جهان شکست
شاخ جوان برید و در آب روان شکست

شاخي که سنگ در کف او حکم شیشه داشت
بر سنگ شیشه چون شکند آن چنان شکست

صد مرغ بخت در سر او سایه کرده بود
نازک دل از عقوبت مرگ گران شکست

سیمرغ آشیانه ي عدل و امان پرید
بازار سکّه خانه ي نقد روان شکست

رفت آن نگار همچو صبا از کنار من
مکنونه را ز آه، رخ آسمان شکست

Our garden's glory, it has been decreed, has shattered,
that young branch, cut off, drop-
                           ping in a brook, has shattered.

ea

Although in his strong hands
                    a stone would smash like glass,
   like a stone smashes glass, it is he who has shattered.

ea

Although a hundred wings of fortune shielded him,
   his fragile heart, that death
                    had weighed upon, has shattered.

ea

Out of our nest of order, the *simurgh* has flown.
   The bank of the bazaar,
                    the counting house, has shattered.

ea

The image of my heart has gone like morning wind
   and with Maknuna's sighs the shining sky has shattered.

Nodira

Nodira

Ul nadurkim, boshi sakson, jismi o'ttiz, poyi bir,
Joni to'rt yuz, aql o'ndur, fahmi ellik benazir.
Jomi o'ymaslikki xat olmish qo'liga toabad,
Yoshirubdur o'zini abjad ichrakim ul dirpazir.

A Riddle

How many heads does he have? Eight-
y. Bodies? Thirty. Feet? Just one.
Four hundred souls. Ten minds. And fif-
ty intellects, each matched by none.
A goblet will last longer if
no name has been engraved on it,
So it is good his has been hid-
den with *abjad*. It will live on.

Uvaysiy

نتظارم بر تو اي سرو خرامانم، بيا
جان به كف ايستاده ام، برخيز، جانانم، بيا

چند از ناز و تغافل تند مي راني سمند
مردمي كن، پاي نه در چشم حيرانم، بيا

صبح وصل من ز خورشيد جمالت نور داشت
شام هجران تيره شد، اي ماه تابانم، بيا

بي تو در كنج ندامت درد هجران مي كشم
وارهان، اي سرو ناز، از درد هجرانم، بيا

چشم خواب آلود من راحت ندارد بي رخت
تا بياسايد دمي مژگان به مژگانم، بيا

اي بهار ناز، چون گل هاي باغ از رفتنت
چاك چاك است از گريبان تا به دامانم، بيا

سرو دلجويت گر از گل زار دامن مي كشد
در رياض جويبار ديده بنشانم، بيا

چشم حيرانم پر طاووس انشا مي كند
همچو گل بي پرده، اي رشك گلستانم، بيا

از خيال زلف او مكنونه پر آشفته ام
ساعتي بر پرسش حال پريشانم، بيا

I wait for you, my sweetly stepping cypress, come.
   I stand here, heart in hand. Arise, my soul's soul, come.

      ❧

It is so long since you,
         so skittishly, would spur your steed.
   Setting your soles upon my eyes,
          still looking for you, come.

      ❧

What I met in the morning was
         the sun of your bright beauty.
   Your absence in the evening dark-
          ens me, my soft moon, come.

      ❧

I am bereft, heartbroken, in
         this nook with my regrets.
   Save me, my sweet, proud cypress, from
          this separation, come.

      ❧

These weary eyes won't sleep without the sight of you.
   Eyelash to eyelash, soothe them for a moment, come.

      ❧

Since your departure from this garden, O sweet spring,
   I have been torn apart like all its petals. Come.

      ❧

I watch the meadow, by the riv-
         er, in the garden, for
   that cypress who is so solicitous to come.

      ❧

Looking for you, my eyes
                   see peacock feathers everywhere.
   O open flower, bringing col-
                  our to this garden, come.

            ۺ

Ask me about my mournfulness.
               My mind in disarray,
   thinking about a lock of hair,
             Maknuna asks you, come.

Nodira

Zamona kulfatidin bu koʻngul dogʻ oʻldi, dogʻ oʻldi,
Bu charxi bemuruvvatdin koʻngul dogʻ oʻldi, dogʻ oʻldi.

Jarohat boʻldi bagʻrim tigʻi bedodi raqiblardin,
Bu koʻtohfahm mardumdin koʻngul dogʻ oʻldi, dogʻ oʻldi.

Bu gulzori fano ichra mahali bexalal yoʻqtur,
Hamesha zaxmi xorodin koʻngul dogʻ oʻldi, dogʻ oʻldi.

Fano mardumlarini sirridin hech kimsa yoʻq ogah,
Qabihguftor mardumdin koʻngul dogʻ oʻldi, dogʻ oʻldi.

Koʻngul qoni farogʻi diydadin bir lahza band oʻlmas,
Vujudim iztirob aylab koʻngul dogʻ oʻldi, dogʻ oʻldi.

Turubdur bagʻrim ichra qon misoli gʻuncha, naylarman,
Ochilmay gulsifat ushbu koʻngul dogʻ oʻldi, dogʻ oʻldi.

Soʻzimdin xotiring uzra gumone oʻzga yetkurma
Ki, izhor aylamay naylay, koʻngul dogʻ oʻldi, dogʻ oʻldi.

Men rasvoyi olamdin mabodo eʼtiroz etma,
Takallum birla shod ayla, koʻngul dogʻ oʻldi, dogʻ oʻldi.

Koʻngulni otashin bejo qilibdur nutqi guftori,
Qayu bogʻ andalibidin koʻngul dogʻ oʻldi, dogʻ oʻldi.

Bu soʻzni ayladi barpo ajab gustohlik birla,
Maloli xotir oʻlgʻaymu, koʻngul dogʻ oʻldi, dogʻ oʻldi.

Ajab ashʼori mavzun bogʻladi Uvaysiy hasaddinkim,
Umarxon zufununekim, koʻngul dogʻ oʻldi, dogʻ oʻldi.

Time and its tribulations, this
          is why my heart is burnt, is burnt.
     The unrelenting turn of it
          is why my heart is burnt, is burnt.

                         ❧

The barbs of those who are against
          me wound these arms that would embrace.
     The backwardness of people, that
          is why my heart is burnt, is burnt.

                         ❧

Nobody has a moment in
          this field of flowers that are fleet-
     ing. Thorns, that keep on pricking me,
          are why my heart is burnt, is burnt.

                         ❧

Nobody knows the secrets of
          the self-annihilated ones.
     The ones who say things bluntly, they
          are why my heart is burnt, is burnt.

                         ❧

The non-stop bleeding of my heart
          is overflowing through my eyes.
     My body is in agony.
          My heart is burnt, is burnt.

                         ❧

How can I do a thing when buds
       of blood have sprung up in my breast?
This rose-like soul of mine won't bloom.
       My heart is burnt, is burnt.

              ੨৯

Don't think that I would say a word
       complaining of my love for you.
How can I stop myself, though, from
       sighing? My heart is burnt, is burnt.

              ੨৯

Don't turn your back on me, I beg
       you, though the world is mocking me.
I will be happy if I hear
       you speak. My heart is burnt, is burnt.

              ੨৯

Your reasoning and rhetoric
       have cast my heart upon the fire.
Which of the garden's nightingales
       is why my heart is burnt, is burnt?

              ੨৯

Those words were blurted out to me
       with such amazing callousness.
Is it so easy not to think
       of me? My heart is burnt, is burnt.

              ੨৯

Uvaysiy, emulating, makes
    amazing, well-made verse in awe
of Umar Khan, a master of
    two arts. My heart is burnt, is burnt.

Uvaysiy

اي سرو ناز تند مرو، سوي من بيا
داغ دلم شكفته، به سير چمن بيا

موزون قدان بر طرف چمن كرده انجمن
اي سرو خوش خرام در اين انجمن بيا

تا چند تلخ كام به هجر تو زيستن
شهدم چشان از آن لب شكرشكن بيا

آيينه‌ي خيال به صيقل رسانده‌ام
در انتظارم، اي صنم سيم تن، بيا...

در كنج هجر نيست چو مكنونه تنگ دل
اي جلوه‌ات بهار طراز چمن بيا

Into this orchard, O sweet cypress, come.
  Slowly, in my scorched heart a scar is open, come.

                              ❧

Those who are tall and graceful have
                              all gathered in the orchard.
  O sweetly stepping cypress, to
                              be one among them, come.

                              ❧

I have a bitter taste of absence in my mouth.
  Some honey from those lips that speak so sweetly, come.

                              ❧

I have made my imagination's mirror shine.
  I wait for my belov-
                              ed, silver-bodied one to come.

                              ❧

Nobody's heart is as bereft as is Maknuna's.
  O spring, to see you ornament this orchard, come.

Nodira

Ul nadurkim, ikki daryoyi ajab xunxordur,
El halokin qasdiga mavj urmishin ko'rdum bukun.
Ul na qushdurkim uyosida, bolalar tashqari,
Don berur vaqtidagi tolpinmishin ko'rdum bukun.

$$ * $$

Ul nadurkim, bir kelin o'zi cho'tur,
Yetti qat parda ichida misli hur.

Two Riddles

Two rivers are what these are, that
      are thirsty, but for blood,
    two torrents, wanting to lay waste,
         and these are what I saw today.

Two birds are also what these are,
       in nests, but restless, they
    fling grain at fledglings that have gone,
        and these are what I saw today.

                 ❧

She is a bride. She has
         a beadiness that she is hid-
Ing under seven veils,
       but she is *houri*-like inside.

Uvaysiy

91

بی تو می سوزد دل ویران ما
پای نه در دیده ی حیران ما

ما کباب آتش عشق توییم
می چکد خونابه از مژگان ما

ما و وصف حسن آن گل چهره نیست
غیر از این، مکنونه در دیوان ما

❧

کف ما نادره جز ساغر حسرت نمی گیرد
ز آتش اشتعال شمع ما رفعت نمی گیرد
ز آب آیینه ی ما هیچ اگر صورت نمی گیرد
مزاج فکر ما با گرم و سرد الفت نمی گیرد
هوایی نیست بیدل سرزمین بی کلاهان را

Your absence burns this ruined heart of ours.
   Step on these restless eyes of ours.

                        ❧

We are charred meat in your love's fire.
   So much blood drips from each eyelash of ours.

                        ❧

Us and our praise of him, his face a rose,
   Maknuna, nothing but for these
                        in this divan of ours.

                        ❧

This goblet of our grief
                and only this has had our hand upon it.
For all the fire there is,
                our candle has not had a flame upon it.
For all the water we have washed it with,
                our mirror has not had a face upon it.
Whatever we are thinking, if the time
                is hot or cold has no effect upon it.
There is no more ambition, Bedil, in
                the land of those who stand bareheaded.

Nodira

93

Jismimi rishtasi, ey ishq, o'shal toba fido,
Aylayin ashkimi ham ul guli seroba fido.

Boshimi sajdadin ar olmasam, ey xalq, ne bok,
Aqlimi ayladim ul g'amzayi mehroba fido.

Sokin o'lsam umr boricha aning hasratida,
Zarfi siymin badan ul shevayi siymoba fido.

Barham aylab ko'zum uyqusini, bedorlig'im
Vaslida nargisini afsun etan xoba fido.

Boqishing ko'ngluma orom, so'zing – jonimg'a,
Kulushing – giryamakim, men bo'lay ahboba fido.

Qilma nomus, meni xirqayi jo'lida ko'rub,
Eyki, nozukbadan, ustingdari sinjoba fido.

Vaysiy, ash'ori bugun nuktayi asroring aro
Muxtasar ham mutaassir duri noyoba fido.

To that round moon, O Love, may my
        innermost being be devoted.
    To that upstanding flower, may
            my weeping also be devoted.

                        ⸙

So what, O people, if I don't
        lift up my forehead from the earth?
    This *mihrab* makes me merry, to
            which all my thinking is devoted.

                        ⸙

May I be longing all my life
        for my beloved. And
    to that one's whims, may the white chal-
        ice of my body be devoted.

                        ⸙

My vigil means my eyes do not
        know sleep. It is the dream
    that the narcissus was enchant-
            ed by to which I am devoted.

                        ⸙

One glance is balsam to my heart,
        one word is to my soul,
    one smile is to my tears. To my
            companions, may I be devoted.

                        ⸙

Don't be dismayed to see me in
    a *khirqa*, seeming crazy. To
that noble raiment on you, O
    fine-bodied one, I am devoted.

              ❧

The art of poetry, that is
    amongst your mysteries, to its
succinct, affecting pearls of wit,
    may I, Uvaysiy, be devoted.

Uvaysiy

Ul shakar labki jondin aziz,
Kimki yo'q ondin aziz, ondin aziz.
Keldi ashraf barcha olam ahlidin.
Yo'qturur dunyoda insondin aziz.

Yo rab, bu savod ishqida sodiq bo'lg'ay.
Iqbol bayozig'a muvofiq bo'lg'ay.
Ishq ahlining xotiri bo'lib xush andin.
Maqbuli tabiati xaloyiq bo'lg'ay.

More than the soul is, those sweet lips are dear.
Who is more dear than him? Is anyone more dear?
Into the world he came, the noblest of all crea-
Tures. Than a human being, nothing is more dear.

ی

O God, that I love wisdom, be it so.
That white luck waits upon me, be it so.
That what I write delights love's devotees
And every living creature, be it so.

Nodira

Ki bulbul nola, afg'on aylamakni mendin o'rgandi,
Vujudin sham'i so'zon aylamakni mendin o'rgandi.

Borib sahroga, qon bag'rimdin izhor ayladim bir kun,
Falak bag'rin qizil qon aylamakni mendin o'rgandi.

Shafaq xun bo'lg'usi, dil, yor mehri gar nihon bo'lsa,
Samo gulguni domon aylamakni mendin o'rgandi.

Ko'rub abro' hiloling, jon fido qildim jamolingga,
Ul oy husniga qurbon aylamakni mendin o'rgandi.

Fig'onkim, g'am tarog'i xasta ko'nglum resh-resh etti,
Sanam zulfin parishon aylamakni mendin o'rgandi.

Seni izlarman andoqkim, quyosh diydorin izlarda,
Kezib tun-kun, shitobon aylamakni mendin o'rgandi.

Qanoat qildi Vaysiy, topti dildin gavhari nazmin,
Sadaf ham durri g'alton aylamakni mendin o'rgandi.

Sighing and crying, that is what
      the nightingale has learned from me.
    Melting its tallow, that is what
      the candle too has learned from me.

ê

I went into the wilderness
      and spread my bloodstained arms out wide.
    Reddening when it hugs the earth
      the evening sky has learned from me.

ê

Dawn will be blood-red, heart, if my
      beloved's loveliness is seen.
    Bundling roses in its skirt
      the morning sky has learned from me.

ê

To see the crescent of an eye-
      brow, I have sacrificed my soul.
    Being consumed by beauty, that
      is what the moon has learned from me.

ê

Wailing and pain, their push and pull,
      have torn this ailing heart to shreds.
    The high hemp letting down its hair
      is what that plant has learned from me.

ê

101

Seeking to see you is the same
  as seeking to behold the sun.
 Day after day, hotfooting it
   is what the sun has learned from me.

      ☄

Uvaysiy, patiently, has scooped
  up from her heart this gem of verse.
 Making so nacreous a thing
   is what the pearl has learned from me.

Uvaysiy

May ichsang, ey ko'ngul, eldin nihon ich,
Labi yodi bila may royigon ich.

Agar g'amdin xalos o'lmoq tilarsen,
Surohiydek sharobi arg'uvon ich.

Ko'ngul, shodob eding vasli mayidin,
Labidin ayru tushding emdi qon ich.

Kirib mayxonaga g'amdin amon top,
Damo-dam jom tut, may har zamon ich.

Mayi nob el iyoriga mahaqdur
Uzingni aylamakka imtihon ich.

Budur mazmuni mavji bodai nob
Ki sahbo piyrni aylar javon ich.

Senga, ey Nodira, jomi muhabbat
Chu sundi soqiyi shirin zabon, ich.

Drink wine, O heart, in hiding, if you want to drink.
  Drink freely, to the lips that you remember, drink.

                          ♨

If what you wish for is your suffering to end,
  drink wine as those decanters purpled by it drink.

                          ♨

Heart, you were happy when you would be one with wine.
  No longer on his lips, now blood is what you drink.

                          ♨

Go to an inn. There you are safe from suffering.
  To moment after moment, toast a glass and drink.

                          ♨

The righteous have the right to pour a glass of pure,
  pure wine. To make yourself
                          what it will make you, drink.

                          ♨

This is a tale awash with wine, a wine so true
  those who are old are young again who drink it. Drink.

                          ♨

A glass to you, Nodira, that is full of fondness,
  as sweet and silky-tongued as that cupbearer, drink.

Nodira

Ma'shuq ahlidin vasl ramzini so'rsam, o'ldirur,
                                    so'rmasam o'lam,
Dardni ahlig'a ishq do'konini qursam, o'ldirur,
                                    qurmasam o'lam.

Rashk jabrina qo'yma, ey ajal, bo'lsa hamnishin
                                    yor g'ayr ila,
Dargohida men tinmay it bo'lib hursam, o'ldirur,
                                    hurmasam o'lam.

Sabr etmavimdin yo'qtur ilojim, istasam ani
                                    toki ro'zu shab,
Ko'-bako' bo'lib men ham darbadar yursam, o'ldirur,
                                    yurmasam o'lam.

Sog'inibduman, bo'libon yiroq, yor deb edi:
                                    "Aylag'ril hazar!"
Gul yuzin bugun oldig'a borib ko'rsam, o'ldirur,
                                    ko'rmasam o'lam.

Mendin or etar, xoru zor etar, foni dunyodin
                                    ushbu jon ketar,
Vaysiyi g'arib rangi sarg'ayib tursam, o'ldirur,
                                    turmasam o'lam.

They kill me, those true lovers, if I ask
      their meeting's meaning. If I don't, I die.
They kill me, those who suffer, if I set
      a stall of love out. If I don't, I die.

                    ஐ

Don't torture me, O death, with jealousy,
      if my beloved sits beside another.
He kills me if I whine outside his door,
      like a lost dog. And if I don't, I die.

                    ஐ

The only thing to do, if I want him,
      is patiently to wait until the dawn.
He kills me if I wander to and fro,
      like an old tramp. And if I don't, I die.

                    ஐ

The reason I was absent for so long
      was my beloved said to me, "Be gone!"
He kills me if I come to gaze upon
      his rosy cheeks. And if I don't, I die.

                    ஐ

He shuns me. He humiliates me. My
      spirit is fleeing from this fleeting world.
He kills me if I keep on being pale.
      And if, poor Vaysiy, if I don't, I die.

Uvaysiy

Nigori gulbadanimni tushumda ko'rsam edi,
Labi shakarshikanimni tushumda ko'rsam edi.

Ko'z ochmayin g'amida ro'zg'orim o'tquchidur,
Ki yori siymtanimni tushumda ko'rsam edi.

Chu davri rohatim o'tti zihi saodat edi,
Murodi jonu tanimni tushumda ko'rsam edi.

G'amida shona kabi chok-chokdur ko'nglim,
Ki, kokili Xo'tanimni tushumda ko'rsam edi.

Yuzi gulu qadi shamshod, ko'zlari nargis,
Bahori yosumanimni tushumda ko'rsam edi.

Jafoi hajr bila ko'ksumi nigor qilay,
Nigohi sehr fanimni tushumda ko'rsam edi.

Labimg'a keldi aning vaslini tilab jonim,
Balo o'ti figanimni tushumda ko'rsam edi.

Hamisha bulbuli tab'im fig'onu zor etar,
Ki, orazi chamanimni tushumda ko'rsam edi.

Firoqi Nodira ko'nglumg'a dog'lar qo'ydi,
Amiri safshikanimni tushumda ko'rsam edi.

My picture of a rose, I wish
                    that I would see him in a dream.
    My sugar-breaker's lips, I wish
                        that I would see them in a dream.

                          ❧

I shut my eyes all day, in pain,
                        without the silver shape
    of my companion. I wish
                    that I would see him in a dream.

                          ❧

The easy days are over, their
                    long string of joys. The will that is
    my body's and my soul's, I wish
                    that I would see it in a dream.

                          ❧

This heart of mine, in agony,
                    is ripped to shreds. A wisp
    of hair with Khotan's scent, I wish
                        that I would see it in a dream.

                          ❧

My tall tree, with a flower's face,
                    with his narcissus eyes,
    my jasmine in the spring, I wish
                    that I would see him in a dream.

                          ❧

Oh, I will daub my breast with what
                              it is to be bereft.
    His eye, adept at spells, I wish
                        that I would see it in a dream.

                              ❧

My soul is in my mouth from want-
                              ing to be one again.
    That fire that makes me scream, I wish
                              that I would see it in a dream.

                              ❧

The nightingale that I am, nat-
                              urally, will forever cry.
    My garden, facing me, I wish
                        that I would see it in a dream.

                              ❧

So far apart from my Amir,
                        Nodira, my line-breaker, there
    are mountains on my heart. I wish
                        that I would see him in a dream.

Nodira

Ul na qushdurkim, qanoti uch erur,
Jismi bir ammo o'zi ellik turur.

﷽

Ul nadurkim, poyi yo'q, yursa boshi birla yurar,
Yurganida xok surmay, oncha ustolik qilar.

Two Riddles

It is a bird, so ultra-light, it has three wings,
One body, though it seems like fifty when it sings.

❧

This one (legs, none) goes head-
first, head down on the ground,
Though it goes smoothly over it
and skilfully around.

Uvaysiy

Kel, dahrni imtihon etib ket,
Sayri chamani jahon etib ket.

Bedardlaring jafolaridin
Faryod chekib, fig'on etib ket.

Dunyo chamanini bulbulisen,
Gul shoxida oshiyon etib ket.

Ey ashk, ko'zimni maktabidin
Hayrat sabaqin ravon etib ket.

Olam chamaniki bevafodur,
Bir oh bila xazon etib ket.

Ushshoq maqomi bo'stondur,
Azmi rahi bo'ston etib ket.

Maqsad na edi, jahona kelding?
Kayfiyatini bayon etib ket.

Fosh etma ulusqa ishq sirrin,
Ko'ngulda ani nihon etib ket.

Kel, ishq yo'lida ko'zlaringni,
Ey Nodira, durfishon etib ket.

Come, that you try the time this is, then go.
  Admire the garden of the earth, then go.

꧁

Being betrayed by an unburdened heart,
  let out a cry, a groan, then go.

꧁

A nightingale in this world's garden, build
  a nest upon a budding branch, then go.

꧁

O tears, sit in the schoolroom of the eyes,
  spill out, surprised by what you learn, then go.

꧁

This garden is unfaithful, anyway,
  so make it autumn with a sigh, then go.

꧁

The venerable status of a lover
  is what to strive towards, then go.

꧁

What is it you are on the earth to do?
  Do it and do it well, then go.

꧁

Show no one the intrinsic truth of love,
   show it to your own soul, then go.

ة

Come, on the way of love, let rubies, O
   Nodira, burst out of your eyes, then go.

Nodira

Qil amon, yo rab, aduvlar mojarosidin meni,
Saqlag'il osiy bu mardumning izosidin meni,
Ser ayla lutfi sultonlar atosidin meni,
Qil judo bul baxt-u tolelar qarosidin meni,
Qutqar, ey xonim, Hasan boqqol balosidin meni,
Qilg'on ul behuda ham jabr-u jafosidin meni.

Koshg'ar yurti buzuldi — keldi, berdim xonumon.
Bosh suqarg'a joy topolmay yurgan erkan bemakon,
Yaxshilik qildim, uyimga, etmadim dod-u fig'on,
Chiqmayin joyi imomdin, ayladi bag'rimni qon.
Qutqar, ey xonim, Hasan boqqol balosidin meni,
Qilg'on ul behuda ham jabr-u jafosidin meni.

Ul mudarris sotti deb, soldi bu ko'nglumga g'ubor,
Oxiri bo'ldi alar kori qoshingda oshkor,
Rahm etib, arzimga yetting sen, deding: "Ey Tunqator,
Yo'q zamonimda mening zo'rliq!" — deding, ey shahriyor,
Qutqar, ey xonim, Hasan boqqol balosidin meni,
Qilg'on ul behuda ham jabr-u jafosidin meni.

Qozilar oldida berdim o'n iki tillosini,
Yona besh tilloni berdim, men pulni foydosini,
Rozi qildi qozilar, man ayladi, ig'vosini,
Yona chiqmas joyidin, yalg'on qilur da'vosini,
Qutqar ey xonim, Hasan boqqol balosidin meni,
Qilg'on ul behuda ham jabr-u jafosidan meni...

O Lord, from all my enemies'
        endeavours, safeguard me,
From all I suffer from, from sin-
        ful people, safeguard me.
From all the sultans' plenitude
        of grace, replenish me,
From these black bonds of bad luck, from
        this fate, unfetter me.
Hasan the hawker, from this bane
        of mine, deliver me,
This burden and this anguish, O
        my Khan, deliver me.

He had come here from Kashgar, home-
        less, I gave him a home.
Nobody, on his wanderings,
        had had a bed for him.
I did a good deed, in my home,
        I didn't howl at him.
And now he acts like my imam
        and does my heart great harm.
Hasan the hawker, from this bane
        of mine, deliver me,
This burden and this anguish, O
        my Khan, deliver me.

A mullah was the seller. Well,
        he said so, to confuse
Me. You, though, saw things clearly and,
        to my suit to you, whose
Mercy is endless, said, "O you,
        who watch the midnight hours,
In my reign, no one suffers." So
        you said, O Shah of ours.

Hasan the hawker, from this bane
       of mine, deliver me,
This burden and this anguish, O
       my Khan, deliver me.

I gave him twelve gold pieces. There
       were judges there to see.
I gave five more, as interest,
       in cash, ungrudgingly.
The judges closed the case, were clear
       he has no tenancy.
And still he will not leave. He has
       made up another plea.
Hasan the hawker, from this bane
       of mine, deliver me,
This burden and this anguish, O
       my Khan, deliver me.

Uvaysiy

Bevafodur bu jahon sudu ziyon barcha abas,
Kim g'amu ayshu bahor ila xazon barcha abas.

Bo'lma andishai savdosi bila sargardon,
Yo'qu bori g'amidin vahmu gumon barcha abas.

Topmasa yor janobig'a sharaf birla qabul,
Ohu faryoding ila sho'ru fig'on barcha abas.

Bo'lmasa oshiqa gar yor visoli maqsud,
Orzui havasi jonu jahon barcha abas.

Fugaro holig'a gar boqmasa har shoh, anga
Hashmatu saltanatu raf'atu shon barcha abas.

Shoh uldurku, raiyatga tarahhum qilsa,
Yo'q esa qoidai amnu amon barcha abas.

Nodira, bo'lmasa gar ishq o'tini ta'siri,
Alami zohir ila dog'i nihon barcha abas.

The losses and the gains, on this
                    inconstant earth, are all in vain,
    the pleasures and the pains, in spring
                    and in the autumn, all in vain.

                    ❧

Don't be absorbed by all the bus-
                    iness that to be in love brings up.
    The make-believe of what might be
                    and might not be is all in vain.

                    ❧

If they don't have a hearing in
                    the court of the Companion,
    those sighs of yours, those screams, the clam-
                    our of your cries are all in vain.

                    ❧

If union for you with your
                    beloved one is not to be,
    belongings, more and more, that you
                    are tempted by, are all in vain.

                    ❧

If the well-being of the poor
                    isn't important to a shah,
    the splendours of his sultanate
                    and stateliness are all in vain.

                    ❧

A shah shows mercy. Mercy shows
                    he is a shah. If he shows none,
      how stable, how secure his reign
                    may seem to be is all in vain.

                    ❧

Nodira, if the inner fire
            of love has no effect upon
      this superficial world, the scars
                    we see from it are all in vain.

Nodira

هیچ میدانی که باز این گردش اختر چه کرد؟
هیچ میدانی که دور چرخ دون پرور چه کرد؟

هیچ میدانی که این نادان دانشمندکُش،
از حسد با جان دانشمند بحر و بر چه کرد؟

هیچ میدانی که این هندوی بازیگر چه ساخت؟
هیچ میدانی که این بدخوی و بدگوهر چه کرد؟

Do you not know what that star, trans-
                    iting its time, has done?
  Do you not know what the malign
                alignment of its time has done?

                        ❧

Do you not know what that one, to
                that boundless scholar, what
  that scholar-killer, ignoram-
                us as he is, has done?

                        ❧

Do you not know what that one, with
                his Hindu tricks, has conjured up?
  Do you not know what that ill temp-
                ered and ill-natured one has done?

Nodira

127

Voqeoti Muhammad Alixon

History Of Muhammad Ali Khan

Uvaysiy

Bugun, ey do'stlar, farzandi jononimni sog'indim,
Gado bo'lsam, ne ayb, ul shohi davronimni sog'indim.

Musofirman, g'aribman, bekasu ham benavodurman,
Vujudim darda to'ldi, emdi darmonimni sog'indim.

Tilimning zikriyu ko'nglimni fikri, yaxshi farzandim,
Azizim, yolg'uzim, davlatli sultonimni sog'indim.

Kecha-kunduz yo'lig'a muntazirdurman, tikarman ko'z,
Kelib holim so'rubon ketsa, mehmonimni sog'indim.

Nasibin uzmadi tangri, ilojin topmag'ay kelsa,
Onam deb bo'lg'usi bag'ri qizil, qonimni sog'indim.

Qorong'u bo'ldi olam ko'zima ushbu judolikdin,
Ko'zu ko'nglum ziyosi, mohi tobonimni sog'indim.

Meni bekas Uvaysiy yig'lag'ayman ro'zi shab tinmay,
Uyimning ziynati, ko'z ravshani, xonimni sog'indim.

Today, my friends, it is my child,
     my dear beloved child I miss.
A beggar I may be, but it
          is that shah of my time I miss.

ﻪ

I am a stranger, an outsid-
     er, miserable and alone.
I am in so much pain from this,
          it is my medicine I miss.

ﻪ

The one my tongue does *zikr* on,
     my heart too, it is my good child,
my dear one and my only one,
          that sultan of my state I miss.

ﻪ

With one eye always on the road,
     all day, all night, I wait for him
to come and ask me how I am.
          It is that visitor I miss.

ﻪ

With no course set for me, may he
     for whom there is no cure come, he
who calls me mother, whose embrace
          is red, my blood, and whom I miss.

ﻪ

The world that is before my eyes,
        seeing his absence, is benighted.
Enlightening my eyes, my heart,
        it is my bright, bright moon I miss.

ِ&

Uvaysiy weeps alone, all night
        and all day. It is that one who,
my khan, brings beauty to my home
        and brightness to my eyes I miss.

Uvaysiy

Ul na kush ko'rinmaskim, shafak bolu pari,
Misli ul raf-raf suvoru bilsangiz, yo'qtur tani,
Voqif erur kecha-kunduz xizmatida to'rt g'ulom,
Qon ilan ermish murassa bul chiyiston maskani.

A Riddle

A bird that is invisible,
      with wings like that white horse's, if
  you know it, feathers like the dawn's,
        it flies to neither field nor flood.

It has four servants who report
      to it, this *chiston*, night and day,
  it has a house, the walls of which
        have all been painted red, with blood.

Uvaysiy

Kelibman dargahingga, shohi xo'bonim, qabul etkil,
Bag'ir qonim bila bul chashmi giryonim qabul etkil.

Umid aylab talab olmoqqa kirdim rohi pokingga,
Yo'lingda aylagan faryodu afg'onim qabul etkil.

Tushubdur boshima savdoyi ishqing, ey shahanshohim,
Alam bozorida bul dardi pinhonim qabul etkil.

O'tubdur gavhari noyobi umrim toki g'aflatda,
Tazarru zor ilan qilg'on pushaymonim qabul etkil.

Tegibdur novakingdin necha o'q jismim aro pinhon,
Shahidi ishq o'lmoqqa oqan qonim qabul etkil.

Uvaysiy garchi noqobil, kelibdur ostoningg'a,
Fig'onu ohi so'zonini, sultonim, qabul etkil.

May I, O my beloved Shah,
>> who come before you, be accepted,
> and may these weeping eyes, this heart
>> that has been broken, be accepted.

ﻉ

May my intention, as I set
>> out on this righteous way, and, as
> I stumble on it, may my cries
>> of lamentation be accepted.

ﻉ

The business of my heart is on
>> my head now, O my Shah of Shahs.
> In misery's bazaar, may these
>> woes I have hidden be accepted.

ﻉ

That pearl of mine, that priceless one,
>> has passed away, while I was heed-
> less. I implore of you that my
>> remorse for this may be accepted.

ﻉ

The arrows of your eyes have hit
>> my body and are buried in
> it. May my martyrdom for love
>> and all this bleeding be accepted.

ﻉ

137

Although I am unworthy, I,
  have come, my Sultan, to your gates,
 weeping and wailing, with my grief.
  May I, Uvaysiy, be accepted.

Uvaysiy

Айш кун, васли ёр даргузар аст,
Бода паймо, баҳори умр даргузар аст.

Кори худро ба вақт бояд кард,
Фурсати рӯзгор даргузар аст.

Сабр кун, то фараҳ ба даст ояд,
Печу тоби хумор даргузар аст.

Эй фалак, бар ин шукӯҳи худ маноз,
Ин ҳама гирудор даргузар аст.

Такя натвон ба фурсати ҳастӣ,
Ҳамчу боди баҳор даргузар аст.

Дахр ойинаест, Макнуна,
Ҳар ки гардад дучор даргузар аст.

The moment with that one is transitory.
   Wine-giver, spring is transitory.

“▼

Do what you have to do in time.
   The time you have is transitory.

“▼

Wait patiently for happiness to come.
   The want of it is also transitory.

“▼

O destiny, do not be proud.
   All that is done is transitory.

“▼

No one can count on luck in life.
   The spring wind it is like is transitory.

“▼

Maknuna, know this world is like a mirror
   and all those in it merely transitory.

Nodira

Mehnatu alamlarga mubtalo Uvaysiyman,
Qayda dard eli bo'lsa, oshno Uvaysiyman.

Istadim bu olamni, topmadim vafo ahlin,
Barchadin yumub ko'zni muddao Uvaysiyman.

Uz diling taalluqdin, band qil xudo sori,
To degil kecha-kunduz: "Mosivo Uvaysiyman!"

Kechalar fig'onimdin tinmadi kavokiblar,
Arz to samo uzra mojaro Uvaysiyman.

To ko'rib xarobotin ta'na etma, ey zohid,
Bir nafas emas xoli iqtido Uvaysiyman.

Faqr borgohiga qo'ysa gar qadam har kim,
Bosh agar kerak bo'lsa, jonfido Uvaysiyman.

Vaysiy beriyozat deb sahl tutma, ey orif,
Ishq aro nihon dardi bedavo Uvaysiyman.

I am one who is overwhelmed
        by suffering, Uvaysiy,
and anywhere it is, I am
        a friend of it, Uvaysiy.

⁂

I haven't found the faithfulness
        I wanted from the world,
so I have shut my eyes, I am
        assiduous Uvaysiy.

⁂

Let nothing in, to tie your heart
        to it, so you can say
to God, all day and all night, "I
        am unattached Uvaysiy."

⁂

The nights get no rest, no respite,
        from me, my cries, my pleas
up to the skies. The stars, from me,
        from struggling Uvaysiy.

⁂

Say nothing, hermit, if you see
        me in a ruined inn.
Not one breath I do nothing with,
        obedient Uvaysiy.

⁂

If anyone steps into mis-
 ery, if it must be
on someone's head, be it on mine,
 self-martyring Uvaysiy.

     ꙳

O Sufi, do not do me wrong
 and call me careless Vaysiy.
Under this suffering is love,
 I am incurable Uvaysiy.

Uvaysiy

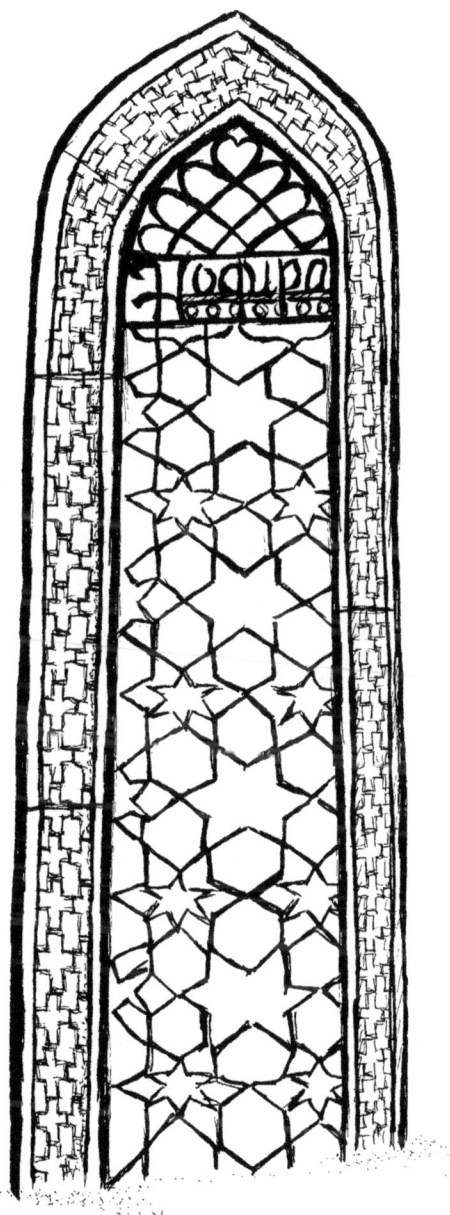

Notes

A Riddle

The answer is a pomegranate.

That Uvaysiy wrote such an outspoken poem about the oppression of women, in harems specifically, while she was living in the palace in Kokand and dependent on the khan's patronage says a lot about her strength of character.

O spring, how sweet it is to see your sapling's stature

Nodira is only one of Mohlaroyim's pen names. She also used the pen names Maknuna and Komila. All the Persian poems in this selection were written under the pen name Maknuna.

Umar Khan, by all accounts, was charming and charismatic. As her khan as well as her husband, and as a fellow poet too, he was a worthy subject for her poems in praise of him, at least at the start of their marriage.

In the *ghazal* tradition, the beloved is often personified as a cypress, for what in English would be their willowy figure, and as the moon or a flower, for their face.

Kamal (کمال), translated as maturity, has the meaning here of the Sufi state of perfectedness.

To the sweet wine of your lips, my

Nodira's love of her husband makes her *ghazals* direct and unambiguous. Uvaysiy, though, didn't like her husband and

149

didn't write anything about him, either when he was alive or after his death. So the subjects of her *ghazals* are much more nebulous. They may be an imaginary person, either as a metaphor for her love of God or simply from her desire to write a *ghazal*.

A *mihrab* is an arched recess in a mosque wall, indicating the direction of Mecca.

Welcome, O envoy of the Sultan, welcome

Umar Khan was often away from the palace, on state business, on month-long hunting trips and on military campaigns. In this *ghazal*, Nodira welcomes a messenger from him and, through the messenger, welcomes her husband himself. Hopefully, the messenger didn't get the wrong message.

In the Koran, a hoopoe was a messenger of Solomon.

Rizwan is an angel in Islam who looks after the garden of paradise.

It was an act of obeisance to the sultan (a khan in this case), to have him put his feet on your eyes.

Two Riddles

The answer to the first riddle is a walnut.

The answer to the second riddle is day and night.

Why are wise men embarrassed by

This *ghazal* is a *mushaira*, a duet or duel between two poets. The first line of the first couplet was written by Umar Khan, the second line by Nodira. The second couplet was written by Nodira, the third couplet by Umar Khan, the fourth couplet by Nodira and so on. Umar Khan wrote the final couplet, so he has the last word. Amiriy is his pen name.

Umar Khan claimed that he was second only to Alisher Navoiy as a poet in Chagatai. Many court poets praised him accordingly. He was a competent poet, but if he was second only to anyone, it was to Nodira and only in their marriage.

That mountain miner is Farhad, who digs through a mountain to get to Shirin. Farhad and Shirin and Layla and Majnun are two of the great love stories in Persian literature.

A *zunnar* was a waistband that non-Muslim men under Muslim rule had to wear, to show they were not Muslim.

A *peri* is a beautiful and benevolent winged spirit in Persian mythology.

It was my heart that love broke out

Hijron, translated as being bereft, is an intense yearning caused by separation from the beloved.

Zikr, used untranslated, is a spiritual practice of repeating phrases in order to remember God.

Spring! So the cypresses

There isn't currently a published edition in Persian script of the Maknuna divan, the collection with most of Nodira's Persian poems. This *ghazal* is one of three in this selection for which only a Cyrillic text was available. Unfortunately, it seems there were grammatical and other errors when the poems were transliterated from Persian script to Cyrillic, but this should not affect the translations.

The hour that it is now on earth

An *iwan* is an open-fronted room or building with an upright rectangular portal.

To be one and be happy, may that be

This is Nodira's response to a *ghazal* by Hafez, the great fourteenth century Persian poet. Nodira uses Hafez's refrain as the basis for her rhyme and refrain (his rhyme and refrain are -*aran yad bad*, hers are -*ad bad*). A translation of Hafez's *ghazal* is in the Appendix.

A *houri* is a beautiful woman in paradise. Compounds like cypress-*houri* are a feature of this literary tradition and are intended to provoke an experience of the extraordinary.

That one who brings such shame upon

There are many different kinds of love expressed, often ambiguously, in the *ghazal* tradition. Love of God, love of a patron, love of a husband, love of a friend, Platonic infatuation and so on. They often vary from one couplet to the next. And more than one kind may be expressed in the same couplet. Uvaysiy adds another kind of love to the list of possibilities. A mother's love for her son.

Savdo, translated here as business, means the process of trading, such as making deals and haggling. It is often used in poetry for the interactions in a romantic relationship.

See the note previously about Farhad.

Thinking of springtime isn't what to do

This *ghazal* shows that Nodira was involved in Sufism, as well as Uvaysiy.

Mansur Hallaj (858–922) was a Sufi mystic who was persecuted for saying *Analhaq* ("I am the Truth"). *Haq* is one of the names of God. He was revered by later Sufis, who understood his revelation as a mystical experience of oneness with God.

Two Riddles

The answer to the first riddle is scissors.

The answer to the second riddle is sleep.

Without you to enjoy this ban-

Umar Khan married three more wives after he had married Nodira, as was customary at the time. The fourth and youngest, Padshah, was renowned for her beauty. Even before meeting her, Umar Khan became obsessed by her and insisted on marrying her. His son, Madali Khan, would later do the same.

Abandonment by the beloved is a standard literary device. It is also an important experience on the mystical Sufi path to God. It is hard, though, not to interpret this *ghazal* and others like it more personally.

See the note previously about the Cyrillic text.

That we, my dear, have faith in all

The inn is an ambivalent and self-deprecating symbol in Sufi poetry. It may mean an actual inn or wineshop, run by non-Muslims, a place of spiritual ruin. It may also mean a Sufi meeting house, a place of spiritual intoxication.

A rose is not a rose unless

See the note previously about Mansur Hallaj.

O rose, the scarlet of my heart

Hadiths are recorded sayings and deeds of the Prophet.

Our garden's glory, it has been decreed, has shattered

Umar Khan died in January 1822, after a short illness. Whatever the illness was, his power to resist it had been weakened, according to his nephew's account of his life, by his heavy drinking and possibly also by the rigours of his military campaigns. He was about 35 and Nodira was 29. She wrote this *ghazal* after his death.

A *simurgh* is a benevolent bird in Persian mythology.

A Riddle

The answer is Plato. The way to solve the riddle is to convert the numbers into letters, using the *abjad* system of assigning numbers to the Arabic alphabet, which was used for counting, the same as Roman numerals, before the current Hindu-Arabic numbers became standard. The numbers go from 1 to 10, then 20, 30, 40 etc to 100, then 200, 300, 400 etc to 1000. For this riddle:

80 = fa
30 = l
1 = ā
400 = t
10 = i
50 = n

The name is Falātin (Falotin in modern Uzbek script), which is an alternative name for Plato in the Islamic world. The riddles were used as educational exercises and this one shows what was expected of the students.

Time and its tribulations, this

This is a response by Uvaysiy to a *ghazal* by Umar Khan, the refrain of which, *bo'ldi*, rhymes with her refrain. The first couplet of his *ghazal* has the words *ajab* (amazing) and *zufunun* (see below), which Uvaysiy uses in the last couplet of hers. Unusually, in her *ghazal*, there isn't a consistent rhyme directly before the refrain.

It may well have been written while Umar Khan was still alive, to impress him. The order of the poems in this selection is a narrative one and not based on any chronological record.

The self-annihilated ones are those who have annihilated the ego and all desires.

Zufunun, translated as a master of two arts, typically refers to someone who is a poet and also a calligrapher or astrologer. In Umar Khan's case, he was a poet and a khan.

Two Riddles

The answer to the first riddle is the eyes.

In love poetry, the beloved's eyes have looks that kill. The lover's eyes, meanwhile, are always looking out for a glimpse of the beloved. The nests are the eyelashes.

The answer to the second riddle is an ear of corn.

Your absence burns this ruined heart of ours

This short *ghazal* is a succinct summary of the aesthetic of Nodira's poetry.

The word translated here, as before, as charred meat, is kebab, which has too many modern connotations in English to be appropriate.

This goblet of our grief

This is the last stanza of a six stanza *mukhammas*. A *mukhammas* is a poem of five-line stanzas. In the first stanza, all five lines rhyme. In the following stanzas, the first four lines rhyme and the fifth line repeats the rhyme of the first stanza. It is written in the style of Bedil (1642-1720), a Mughal poet and the greatest exponent of the later Indian style in Persian poetry. The last line is a direct quote.

Standing bareheaded is a symbol of either a lack of power or a Sufi rejection of it.

To that round moon, O Love, may my

Similar to the previous *ghazal* by Nodira, this can be seen as a summary of the aesthetic of Uvaysiy's poetry. It is addressed to love itself, rather than to a personal beloved. And it includes her devotion to the Sufi way of mystical love, as well as her devotion to poetry.

A *khirqa* is a patchwork Sufi cloak, associated with initiation and the transmission of spiritual knowledge.

More than the soul is, those sweet lips are dear
O God, that I love wisdom, be it so

These two *ruba'iyat* are part of the introduction that Nodira wrote for a collection of her poems under the pen name Komila. A *ruba'i* is a four line poem, rhyming either AABA or AAAA.

Sighing and crying, that is what

The nightingale, the candle and everything else in the poem learn what to do from the poet who has written it.

They kill me, those true lovers, if I ask

Those true lovers may refer to the members of a Sufi lodge.

Being pale is a sign of the anguish of being in love.

My picture of a rose, I wish

Khotan, now in Xinjiang, is an oasis town on an old Silk Roads route, famous for its beauty and for musk.

Two Riddles

The answer to the first riddle is the soul. This riddle also uses the *abjad* system to convert the numbers into letters. For this one:

3 = j
1 = ā
50 = n

Jān (*jon* in modern Uzbek script) means soul. In the translation, the answer is shown in the first line (the original *chistons* have a lot of untranslatable wordplay).

The answer to the second riddle is water.

O Lord, from all my enemies'

A *tarjiband* is a poem in which the last two lines of the first stanza are repeated as a refrain in the following stanzas.

This *tarjiband* is a petition for help by Uvaysiy to Madali Khan. She was living in a house provided for her by Nodira and had given refuge there to a homeless grocer from Kashgar. He had taken over the courtyard for his own use and was abusing her hospitality.

Do you not know what that star, trans-

Only the first three couplets of this *ghazal* were available. Even as a fragment, though, it is worth including.

In the Soviet period, what made Nodira ideologically acceptable, despite being a queen, was her awareness of injustice, her sympathy for the poor and the oppressed. The emphasis on this has continued since then. What is more striking, though, and expressed so starkly here (and more diplomatically in the previous *ghazal*), is that the perpetrator of these injustices, the oppressor whom she criticises, is Madali Khan, her own son.

History Of Muhammad Ali Khan

There isn't currently a published edition of Uvaysiy's complete works and none of her three *dastans* are available. The other two, which tell the stories of Hasan and Husayn, were perhaps too religious to be published in the Soviet period, but the unavailability of this one is inexplicable. Muhammad Ali Khan is the full name of Madali Khan. According to those who have read the *dastan*, Uvaysiy describes his character and his relationship with his mother. She also describes her friendship with Nodira and her esteem for Nodira as a poet.

It starts with praise for Madali Khan, so it was intended as a public poem, for his approval, if not to gain favour for Uvaysiy herself, then perhaps for her son. She wrote 208 lines, then abandoned it. It ends with Madali Khan's army setting out from Kokand on a campaign against Kashgar.

Madali Khan mounted two campaigns against Kashgar, both of which failed. Uvaysiy's son was in the army for at least one of them. It isn't clear which campaign Uvaysiy describes, or if she abandoned the *dastan* because the campaign had failed or for a more personal reason. It is, at least, possible that she started the poem intending to glorify a victory in which her son was involved.

It is to be hoped that the manuscripts of both poets' works, where so many poems are languishing (Uvaysiy's *dastans* and Nodira's Persian poems, among others), will soon be digitised and made available, and that modern critical editions of their complete works will be prepared and published.

Today, my friends, it is my child

This *ghazal* was written while Uvaysiy's son was away in Madali Khan's army, on one of his campaigns to conquer Kashgar. He was killed in battle.

A Riddle

The answer, again, is the soul.

The white horse is the horse Muhammad rode for his Ascension.

The four servants are the eyes, ears, mouth and nose (i.e. seeing, hearing, taste and smell).

The moment with that one is transitory

See the note previously about the Cyrillic text.

Appendix

This is a *ghazal* by Hafez, the great fourteenth century Persian poet, which Nodira wrote a *ghazal* in response to (*To be one and be happy, may that be*).

The Bagh-i-Karan is one of the four famous gardens in Isfahan.

روز وصل دوستداران یاد باد

یاد باد آن روزگاران یاد باد

کامم از تلخی غم چون زهر گشت

بانگ نوش شادخواران یاد باد

گر چه یاران فارغند از یاد من

از من ایشان را هزاران یاد باد

مبتلا گشتم در این بند و بلا

کوشش آن حق گزاران یاد باد

گر چه صد رود است در چشمم مدام

زنده رود باغ کاران یاد باد

راز حافظ بعد از این ناگفته ماند

ای دریغا رازداران یاد باد

Those days of being one, long may they be,
　　long may they be, those days, long may they be.

❧

Tongue toxic, with the sourness of sorrow,
　　those happy drinking songs, long may they be.

❧

Although my friends no longer think of me,
　　a thousand thoughts of them, long may they be.

❧

I got infected in this ward. Disaster!
　　Those righteous ones who strive, long may they be.

❧

A hundred streams are always in my eyes.
　　The Bagh-i-Karan's streams, long may they be.

❧

Hafez's secret still has not been said.
　　Those who keep secrets, ah, long may they be.

Hafez

The Translators

Andrew Staniland is an English poet. He was born in 1959. He spent his childhood in Sheffield, England, and studied Politics at Durham University. Since then, he has worked part time and written poetry. He has published another book of translations, *12 Ghazals By Alisher Navoiy, 14 Poems By Abdulhamid Cho'lpon*, which he did with Aida and another Uzbek translator, Avazkhon Khaydarov. Among his own collections, *A New Diwan (h/t Alisher Navoiy)* is a sequence of short poems inspired by Uzbekistan and Navoiy. *In Couplets* includes a set of English *ghazals* and two sequences of aphorisms, one prompted by Babur's *Baburnama* and the other by Sa'di's *Gulistan*.

Nazeela Elmi is a graduate student. She was born in 1997. She spent her early childhood in the rural province of Faryab in northern Afghanistan. When she was eight, she hosted a children's radio show on Radio Rabia Balkhi in Mazar-e-Sharif. At high school in Kabul, she won gold medals in national and international language competitions. She studied Politics and International Relations at the TED University in Ankara, Turkey, and also spent a semester at Leipzig University, in Germany, on an Erasmus Exchange programme. Nazeela has worked on humanitarian projects, including programmes for Afghan women in Turkey and fundraising for displaced families in Faryab. She has had articles published in English, Turkish and German, and has addressed a UNESCO conference. She is currently waiting to start a Masters programme.

Aidakhon Bumatova is a translator and interpreter. She was born in 1991. She grew up in Samarkand, one of the cities in Uzbekistan where Tajik is widely spoken. She has a PhD in Translation Studies from the Alisher Navoiy Tashkent State University of Uzbek Language and Literature and is currently doing post-doctoral research. She has written over 20 articles on the translation of poetry and has translated several of Navoiy's *ghazals* and Babur's *ruba'iyat* into English. She co-translated the twelve *ghazals* in the book *12 Ghazals By Alisher Navoiy, 14 Poems By Abdulhamid Cho'lpon*.

Acknowledgements

Many thanks for their help to Zebo Abdullazizova, Enjila Bahmanyar, Sevara Dultaeva, Ahmad Farid Elmi, Khaleda Elmi, Sophie Ibbotson, Naima Muminiy, Shakhnoza Mustanova, A'zam Obidov, Go'zal Po'latova, Ziafatullah Saeedi and Nozimabonu Sherbekova.

" I want to thank everybody involved in this, for their support and enthusiasm, which has made it such a joy. Nazeela, especially, in exile from Afghanistan, for her insight and ideas, her friendship and (despite everything else going on) so much fun. Naima, finding time from her law studies in Washington D.C., for getting it right away. Sophie, from Reading to Kokand and back again, for her thoroughly modern graciousness. And Aida, in Tashkent, for answering the call to get the band back together. "

Andrew

12 GHAZALS BY ALISHER NAVOIY, 14 POEMS BY ABDULHAMID CHO'LPON

12 Ghazals By Alisher Navoiy, 14 Poems By Abdulhamid Cho'lpon is a selection of English translations of poems by the fifteenth century poet Alisher Navoiy, Uzbekistan's adopted national poet and the greatest poet in the old Turkic language Chagatai, and the twentieth century poet Abdulhamid Cho'lpon, the greatest poet in modern Uzbek. The English versions are by the English poet Andrew Staniland, with the help of Uzbek translators Aidakhon Bumatova and Avazkhon Khaydarov.

IN COUPLETS

Andrew Staniland's *In Couplets* is a sequence of poems in long, stepped couplets. It starts in London in the autumn of 2020, in lockdown from the Covid pandemic, with protests in Belarus and war in Nagorno-Karabakh. It continues through 2021, with a summer of floods and fires and the fall of Afghanistan to the Taliban, and ends in the spring of 2022, with Russia's assault on Ukraine. There is also a set of ten English *ghazals* and two series of aphorisms, one prompted by Babur's *Baburnama*, the other by Sa'di's *Gulistan*.

12 GHAZALS BY ALISHER NAVOIY, 14 POEMS BY ABDULHAMID CHO'LPON

12 Ghazals By Alisher Navoiy, 14 Poems By Abdulhamid Cho'lpon is a selection of English translations of poems by the fifteenth century poet Alisher Navoiy, Uzbekistan's adopted national poet and the greatest poet in the old Turkic language Chagatai, and the twentieth century poet Abdulhamid Cho'lpon, the greatest poet in modern Uzbek. The English versions are by the English poet Andrew Staniland, with the help of Uzbek translators Aidakhon Bumatova and Avazkhon Khaydarov.

IN COUPLETS

Andrew Staniland's *In Couplets* is a sequence of poems in long, stepped couplets. It starts in London in the autumn of 2020, in lockdown from the Covid pandemic, with protests in Belarus and war in Nagorno-Karabakh. It continues through 2021, with a summer of floods and fires and the fall of Afghanistan to the Taliban, and ends in the spring of 2022, with Russia's assault on Ukraine. There is also a set of ten English *ghazals* and two series of aphorisms, one prompted by Babur's *Baburnama*, the other by Sa'di's *Gulistan*.

A NEW DIWAN (H/T ALISHER NAVOIY)

Andrew Staniland's *A New Diwan (h/t Alisher Navoiy)* is a sequence of 84 short poems, written in long, stepped couplets and inspired by the fifteenth century poet, as well as by Uzbekistan's Silk Road cities, its literature and landscapes. It is a contemplative, non-narrative sequence, to be read a few poems at a time.

Printed in Great Britain
by Amazon